Common CORE Writing to Te...

MW00528012

Table of Contents

Introduction

What Is the Common Core?

The Common Core State Standards are an initiative by states to set shared, consistent, and clear criteria for what students are expected to learn. This helps teachers and parents know what they need to do to help students. The standards are designed to be rigorous and pertinent to the real world. They reflect the knowledge and skills that young people need for success in college and careers.

If your state has joined the Common Core State Standards Initiative, then teachers are required to incorporate these standards into their lesson plans. Students need targeted practice in order to meet grade-level standards and expectations, and thereby be promoted to the next grade.

What Does It Mean to Write to Texts?

One of the most important instructional shifts in the Common Core State Standards is writing to texts, or sources. What exactly does this mean? Haven't standardized assessments always used reading texts as a springboard to writing? Yes, but the required writing hasn't always been DEPENDENT on the key ideas and details in a text.

A prompt that is non-text dependent asks students to rely on prior knowledge or experience. In fact, students could likely carry out the writing without reading the text at all. The writing does not need to include ideas, information, and key vocabulary from the text.

Writing to texts requires students to analyze, clarify, and cite information they read in the text. The writing reveals whether students have performed a close reading, because it is designed to elicit ideas, information, and key vocabulary from the text as well as students' own evidence-based inferences and conclusions. These are all skills that prepare them for the grades ahead, college, the workplace, and real-world applications in their adult daily lives.

An example of a passage with non-text-dependent and text-dependent sample prompts is provided on page 3.

Simple Machines

1. A simple machine is a tool that does work with one movement. It has few or no moving parts and uses energy to do work. A lever, a wedge, a screw, a pulley, and a ramp are all simple machines.

2. You use simple machines all the time, too. If you have opened a door, eaten with a spoon, cut with scissors, or zipped up a zipper, you have used a simple machine.

3. Life would be very different if we did not have machines. Work would be much harder, and playing wouldn't be as much fun.

Standard	Sample Prompt: Non-Text Dependent	Sample Prompt: Text Dependent
W.2.1 (Opinion/ Argument)	Do you prefer zippers, buttons, buckles, or another type of fastener for your clothing? Why?	The author makes three claims in the last paragraph. Choose one and tell whether you agree or disagree. Support your opinion with facts from the text.
W.2.2 (Informative Explanatory)	Think about a machine you have used to do a task. How did you use it? How did using the machine make the task easier?	Explain what a simple machine is. Use details from the text to support your explanation.
W.2.3 (Narrative)	Write a story in which a character invents a machine that no one has seen or heard of before.	Imagine that all the machines mentioned in the passage disappeared for twenty-four hours. Write a journal entry about how your life was different that day and what you learned.

Using this Book

How Does This Book Help Students?

This book is organized into three main sections: Writing Mini-Lessons, Practice Texts with Prompts, and Rubrics and Assessments. All mini-lessons and practice pages are self-contained and may be used in any order that meets the needs of students. The elements of this book work together to provide students with the tools they need to be able to master the range of skills and application as required by the Common Core.

1. Mini-Lessons for Opinion/Argument, Informative/ Explanatory, and Narrative Writing

Writing mini-lessons prepare students to use writing as a way to state and support opinions, demonstrate understanding of the subjects they are studying, and convey real and imagined experiences. The mini-lessons are organized in the order of the standards, but you may wish to do them with your class in an order that matches your curriculum. For each type of writing the first mini-lesson covers responding to literature, while the second mini-lesson models how to respond to informational text.

Each mini-lesson begins with a lesson plan that provides step-by-step instruction.

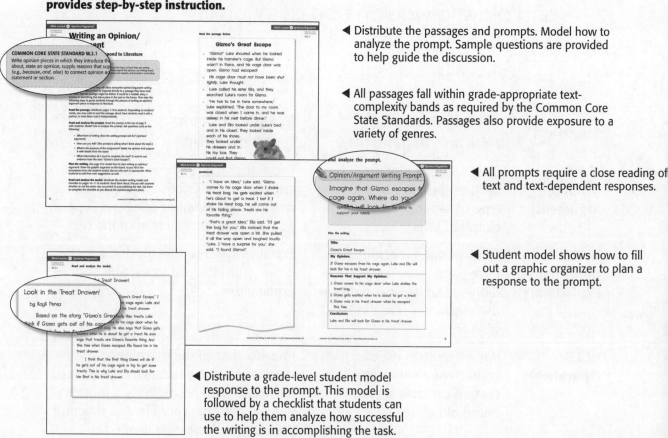

◀ Distribute the passages and prompts. Model how to analyze the prompt. Sample questions are provided to help guide the discussion.

◀ All passages fall within grade-appropriate text-complexity bands as required by the Common Core State Standards. Passages also provide exposure to a variety of genres.

◀ All prompts require a close reading of text and text-dependent responses.

◀ Student model shows how to fill out a graphic organizer to plan a response to the prompt.

◀ Distribute a grade-level student model response to the prompt. This model is followed by a checklist that students can use to help them analyze how successful the writing is in accomplishing the task.

2. Practice Texts with Prompts

Passages and prompts provide students with real experience writing to a text. Each passage is followed by three text-dependent prompts: Opinion/Argument, Informative/Explanatory, and Narrative. On each prompt page, students are also provided with a graphic organizer to help them plan their writing.

You may wish to assign a particular prompt, have students choose one, or have them execute each type of writing over a longer period of time. For each type of writing, you can distribute a corresponding checklist to help students plan and evaluate their writing.

For more information on how to use this section, see page 42.

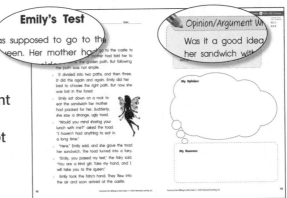

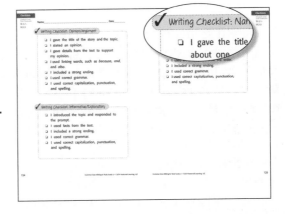

3. Rubrics and Assessments

The section includes Evaluation Rubrics to guide your assessment and scoring of students' responses. Based on your observations of students' writing, use the differentiated rubrics. These are designed to help you conduct meaningful conferences with students and will help differentiate your interactions to match students' needs.

For each score a student receives in the Evaluation Rubrics, responsive prompts are provided. These gradual-release prompts scaffold writers toward mastery of each writing type.

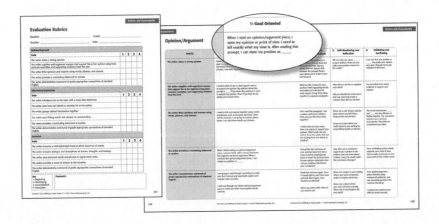

COMMON CORE
STATE STANDARD
W.2.1

Writing an Opinion/ Argument

Mini-Lesson 1: Respond to Literature

> **COMMON CORE STATE STANDARD W.2.1**
> Write opinion pieces in which they introduce the topic or book they are writing about, state an opinion, supply reasons that support the opinion, use linking words (e.g., *because, and, also*) to connect opinion and reasons, and provide a concluding statement or section.

Explain to students that they will often encounter opinion/argument writing prompts that instruct them to respond directly to a passage they have read. Tell them that the passage might be fiction. It could be a realistic story, a fantasy, or something that takes place in the past or the future. Then take the following steps to guide students through the process of writing an opinion/ argument piece in response to literature.

Read the passage. Distribute pages 7–9 to students. Depending on students' needs, you may wish to read the passage aloud, have students read it with a partner, or have them read it independently.

Read and analyze the prompt. Read the prompt at the top of page 9 with students. Model how to analyze the prompt. Ask questions such as the following:

- *What form of writing does the writing prompt ask for?* (opinion/ argument)

- *How can you tell?* (The prompt is asking what I think about the topic.)

- *What is the purpose of the assignment?* (state my opinion and support it with details from the story)

- *What information do I need to complete the task?* (I need to use evidence from the story "Gizmo's Great Escape.")

Plan the writing. Use page 9 to model how to plan writing an opinion/ argument. Draw the graphic organizer on the board. As you fill in the annotations from the student model, discuss why each is appropriate. Allow students to add their own suggestions as well.

Read and analyze the model. Distribute the student writing model and checklist on pages 10–11 to students. Read them aloud. Discuss with students whether or not the writer was successful at accomplishing the task. Ask them to complete the checklist as you discuss the opinion/argument piece.

Read the passage below.

Gizmo's Great Escape

1.   "Gizmo!" Luke shouted when he looked inside his hamster's cage. But Gizmo wasn't in there, and his cage door was open. Gizmo had escaped!

2.   *His cage door must not have been shut tightly,* Luke thought.

3.   Luke called his sister Ella, and they searched Luke's room for Gizmo.

4.   "He has to be in here somewhere," Luke explained. "The door to my room was closed when I came in, and he was asleep in his nest before dinner."

5.   Luke and Ella looked under Luke's bed and in his closet. They looked inside each of his shoes. They looked under his dressers and in his toy box. They could not find Gizmo anywhere.

(continued)

COMMON CORE
STATE STANDARD
W.2.1

(continued)

6. "I have an idea," Luke said. "Gizmo comes to his cage door when I shake his treat bag. He gets excited when he's about to get a treat. I bet if I shake his treat bag, he will come out of his hiding place. Treats are his favorite thing."

7. "That's a great idea," Ella said. "I'll get the bag for you." Ella noticed that the treat drawer was open a bit. She pulled it all the way open and laughed loudly. "Luke, I have a surprise for you," she said. "I found Gizmo!"

Read and analyze the prompt.

Opinion/Argument Writing Prompt

Imagine that Gizmo escapes from his cage again. Where do you think Luke and Ella will look for him first? State your opinion. Then use details from the story to support your ideas.

Plan the writing.

Title:
Gizmo's Great Escape
My Opinion:
If Gizmo escapes from his cage again, Luke and Ella will look for him in his treat drawer.
Reasons That Support My Opinion:
1. Gizmo comes to his cage door when Luke shakes the treat bag.
2. Gizmo gets excited when he is about to get a treat.
3. Gizmo was in his treat drawer when he escaped this time.
Conclusion:
Luke and Ella will look for Gizmo in his treat drawer.

COMMON CORE
STATE STANDARD
W.2.1

Read and analyze the model.

Look in the Treat Drawer!

by Kayli Perez

Based on the story "Gizmo's Great Escape," I think if Gizmo gets out of his cage again, Luke and Ella will look for him first in his treat drawer.

Gizmo the hamster really likes treats. Luke says that Gizmo comes to his cage door when he shakes his treat bag. He also says that Gizmo gets excited when he is about to get a treat. He even says that treats are Gizmo's favorite thing. And this time when Gizmo escaped, Ella found him in his treat drawer.

I think that the first thing Gizmo will do if he gets out of his cage again is try to get some treats. This is why Luke and Ella should look for him first in his treat drawer.

✔ Writing Checklist: Opinion/Argument

❑ The writer gave the title of the story and the topic.

❑ The writer stated an opinion.

❑ The writer gave details from the text to support her opinion.

❑ The writer used linking words, such as *because*, *and*, and *also*.

❑ The writer included a strong ending.

❑ The writer used correct grammar.

❑ The writer used correct capitalization, punctuation, and spelling.

COMMON CORE
STATE STANDARD
W.2.1

Writing an Opinion/ Argument

Mini-Lesson 2: Respond to Informational Text

> **COMMON CORE STATE STANDARD W.2.1**
> Write opinion pieces in which they introduce the topic or book they are writing about, state an opinion, supply reasons that support the opinion, use linking words (e.g., *because*, *and*, *also*) to connect opinion and reasons, and provide a concluding statement or section.

Explain to students that they will often encounter opinion/argument writing prompts that instruct them to respond directly to a passage they have read. Tell them that the passage might be nonfiction. It might be a passage about science or social studies, a how-to passage, a biography or an autobiography, or a digital source. Then take the following steps to guide students through the process of writing an opinion/argument piece in response to an informational text.

Read the passage. Distribute pages 13–15 to students. Depending on students' needs, you may wish to read the passage aloud, have students read it with a partner, or have them read it independently.

Read and analyze the prompt. Read the prompt at the top of page 15 with students. Model how to analyze the prompt. Ask questions such as the following:

- *What form of writing does the writing prompt ask for?* (opinion/argument)

- *How can you tell?* (The prompt is asking what I think about the topic.)

- *What is the purpose of the assignment?* (state my opinion and support it with details from the story)

- *What information do I need to complete the task?* (I need to use evidence from the story "Laura Ingalls Wilder.")

Plan the writing. Use page 15 to model how to plan writing an opinion/argument. Draw the graphic organizer on the board. As you fill in the annotations from the student model, discuss why each is appropriate. Allow students to add their own suggestions as well.

Read and analyze the model. Distribute the student writing model and checklist on pages 16–17 to students. Read them aloud. Discuss with students whether or not the writer was successful at accomplishing the task. Ask them to complete the checklist as you discuss the opinion/argument piece.

Read the passage below.

Laura Ingalls Wilder

1. Laura Ingalls Wilder was born in Wisconsin in 1867. She is famous for the books she later wrote for children about her life growing up.

2. Laura and her family moved west to the prairie when Laura was little. Prairie land is flat and grassy, with few trees. At that time, they were among the first families to settle down there. They were real "pioneers."

3. Laura and her family had to build their own home. They grew or caught their own food. It was a difficult life, especially during the cold winters.

4. Sometimes the family worried they might not survive. They helped one another, however, and made a new life there.

(continued)

(continued)

5. Laura grew up to become a teacher. She married a man named Almanzo, and they had a daughter, Rose.

6. Later on, Rose wanted her mother to write about life growing up. She helped her mother get started, and Laura ended up writing a whole set of books.

7. Her most famous book is *Little House on the Prairie.* Laura tells the story of what life was like for her and her family when she was growing up. Laura, Ma, Pa, and her sisters, Mary and Carrie, had to work hard every day to survive on the prairie. But at night, they did enjoy being together, safe and warm in their little house. The girls often would fall asleep while happily listening to Pa play his fiddle.

8. Laurie died in 1957 at age ninety. Children today continue to read and enjoy her books about her life long ago as a young pioneer.

Read and analyze the prompt.

Opinion/Argument Writing Prompt

Do you think Laura and her family were happy living on the prairie? Why or why not? Support your opinion with evidence from the text and your own ideas.

Plan the writing.

Title:
Laura Ingalls Wilder
My Opinion:
I think Laura and her family were happy living on the prairie even though their life was difficult.
Reason:
The text says they made a new life for themselves on the prairie.
Supporting Details:
1. They had one another to depend on when life was hard.
2. At night they enjoyed being together and being warm and safe in their home.
3. The children were happy as they fell asleep listening to Pa play his fiddle.

COMMON CORE
STATE STANDARD
W.2.1

Read and analyze the model.

Laura and Her Family Were Happy Living on the Prairie

by DeShawn Reynolds

In the text "Laura Ingalls Wilder," I think Laura and her family were happy living on the prairie, even though there weren't many other people around.

The text says that Laura and her family were pioneers. This means that they were one of the first families to settle there. Their life was difficult. They had to grow or catch their own food. They even had to build their own house! But the text says they had one another to depend on for help.

The happiest times for them were at home together at night. The text says that they were glad to be warm and safe in their home. Also, the children enjoyed listening to Pa play his fiddle until they fell asleep.

For these reasons, I think they were happy living on the prairie.

✔ Writing Checklist: Opinion/Argument

- ❏ The writer gave the title of the story and the topic.
- ❏ The writer stated an opinion.
- ❏ The writer gave details from the text to support the opinion.
- ❏ The writer used linking words, such as *because*, *and*, and *also*.
- ❏ The writer included a strong ending.
- ❏ The writer used correct grammar.
- ❏ The writer used correct capitalization, punctuation, and spelling.

COMMON CORE
STATE STANDARD
W.2.2

Writing an Informative/ Explanatory Text

Mini-Lesson 3: **Respond to Literature**

> **COMMON CORE STATE STANDARD W.2.2**
> Write informative/explanatory texts in which they name a topic, supply some facts about the topic, and provide some sense of closure.

Explain to students that they will often encounter informative/explanatory writing prompts that instruct them to respond directly to a passage they have read. Tell them that the passage might be fiction. It could be a realistic story, a fantasy, or something that takes place in the past or the future. Then take the following steps to guide students through the process of writing an informative/explanatory piece in response to literature.

Read the passage. Distribute pages 19–21 to students. Depending on students' needs, you may wish to read the passage aloud, have students read it with a partner, or have them read it independently.

Read and analyze the prompt. Read the prompt at the top of page 21 with students. Model how to analyze the prompt. Ask questions such as the following:

- *What form of writing does the writing prompt ask for?* (informative/ explanatory)

- *How can you tell?* (The prompt is asking me what character traits describe Sun.)

- *What is the purpose of the assignment?* (give an explanation and support it with details from the story)

- *What information do I need to complete the task?* (I need to use evidence from the story "Sun and Wind.")

Plan the writing. Use page 21 to model how to plan writing an informative/ explanatory piece. Draw the graphic organizer on the board. As you fill in the annotations from the student model, discuss why each is appropriate. Allow students to add their own suggestions as well.

Read and analyze the model. Distribute the student writing model and checklist on pages 22–23 to students. Read them aloud. Discuss with students whether or not the writer was successful at accomplishing the task. Ask them to complete the checklist as you discuss the informative/explanatory piece.

COMMON CORE
STATE STANDARD
W.2.2

Read the passage below.

Sun and Wind
(adapted from the fable by Aesop)

1.   Once upon a time, Sun and Wind were arguing about who was stronger. When Sun saw a man walking along the road, she had an idea. "Let's have a contest. Let's see who can make that man take off his coat. Whoever can do this is the strongest."

2.   Wind liked this idea. *All I have to do is blow really hard. The man will get tired of his coat blowing in the breeze and will take it off*, he thought.

3.   "Agreed," said Wind. Sun offered to let Wind go first and then hid behind a cloud.

(continued)

COMMON CORE
STATE STANDARD
W.2.2

(continued)

4.   Wind blew as hard as he could. He tried and tried to blow the coat off the man. But the harder he blew, the tighter the man wrapped the coat around him. "I give up," said Wind. "That man is never going to take off his coat. It's your turn."

5.   Sun came out from behind the cloud. She shone on the man. With her bright rays, she made the day warmer and warmer. The man smiled to himself as he walked along. Soon he took off his coat and tossed it over his shoulder.

6.   It is better to be gentle than forceful.

Common Core Writing to Texts Grade 2 • ©2014 Newmark Learning, LLC

COMMON CORE
STATE STANDARD
W.2.2

Read and analyze the prompt.

Informative/Explanatory Writing Prompt

What words can you use to describe what Sun is like in the story? Use details from the story to explain your answer.

Plan the writing.

Main Points	Details
1. Sun is smart.	She comes up with a plan to show Wind that she is stronger. She figures out a way to make the man take off his coat, so she can win the contest.
2. She is polite.	She offers to let Wind go first.
3. Sun is gentle.	The way she chooses to get the man to take off his coat is gentle and not forceful like the way Wind tries to get him to take off the coat.
Conclusion: Sun is smart, polite, and gentle.	

COMMON CORE
STATE STANDARD
W.2.2

Read and analyze the model.

Sun's Character Traits

by Tara Douglas

In the story "Sun and Wind," Sun is smart, polite, and gentle.

Sun is very smart. At the beginning of the story, Sun and Wind are arguing about who is stronger. It is Sun who comes up with the idea to hold a contest. Then she chooses the contest. She probably already knows how she will win this contest.

Sun is also polite because she lets Wind go first. She is also gentle. Wind uses force to try to get the man to take off the coat. Wind blows as hard as he can. But Sun uses a gentle way. She just shines until it is too warm to wear a coat.

For these reasons, Sun's character traits are that she is smart, polite, and gentle.

✔ Writing Checklist: Informative/Explanatory

❑ The writer introduced the topic and responded to the prompt.

❑ The writer used facts from the text.

❑ The writer included a strong ending.

❑ The writer used correct grammar.

❑ The writer used correct capitalization, punctuation, and spelling.

COMMON CORE
STATE STANDARD
W.2.2

Writing an Informative/ Explanatory Text

Mini-Lesson 4: Respond to Informational Text

> **COMMON CORE STATE STANDARD W.2.2**
> Write informative/explanatory texts in which they name a topic, supply some facts about the topic, and provide some sense of closure.

Explain to students that they will often encounter informative/explanatory writing prompts that instruct them to respond directly to a passage they have read. Tell them that the passage might be nonfiction. It might be a passage about science or social studies, a how-to passage, a biography or an autobiography, or a digital source. Then take the following steps to guide students through the process of writing an informative/explanatory piece in response to an informational text.

Read the passage. Distribute pages 25–27 to students. Depending on students' needs, you may wish to read the passage aloud, have students read it with a partner, or have them read it independently.

Read and analyze the prompt. Read the prompt at the top of page 27 with students. Model how to analyze the prompt. Ask questions such as the following:

- *What form of writing does the writing prompt ask for?* (informative/ explanatory)

- *How can you tell?* (The prompt is asking to compare and contrast the way an adult ladybug looks with the way a larva looks.)

- *What is the purpose of the assignment?* (give an explanation and support it with details from the story)

- *What information do I need to complete the task?* (I need to use evidence from the text "The Lovely Ladybug" and the pictures.)

Plan the writing. Use page 27 to model how to plan writing an informative/ explanatory text. Draw the graphic organizer on the board. As you fill in the annotations from the student model, discuss why each is appropriate. Allow students to add their own suggestions as well.

Read and analyze the model. Distribute the student writing model and checklist on pages 28–29 to students. Read them aloud. Discuss with students whether or not the writer was successful at accomplishing the task. Ask them to complete the checklist as you discuss the informative/explanatory piece.

Read the passage below.

The Lovely Ladybug

1. A ladybug is a small beetle that is usually red with black spots on its back. It has a tiny head and six legs. It also has wings, but they aren't always easy to see.

2. A ladybug has two hard shells on its back. When it is not flying, it tucks its wings under these shells. When it wants to fly, these shells spread apart. Then the ladybug's wings come out from under the shells.

3. A baby ladybug does not look like an adult. It is called a larva. A larva looks like a black caterpillar with spikes on its back and six legs. As it gets older, a larva's body becomes more round like an adult's.

wings

legs

head

antenna

(continued)

Common Core
State Standard

W.2.2

(continued)

4. Farmers like to have ladybugs around because ladybugs eat insects that harm crops. And a single ladybug has a very big appetite. It can eat fifty insects a day!

5. A ladybug stays safe in an interesting way. If it becomes scared, it will play dead! Ladybugs also don't taste good to larger insects and birds. When they see a ladybug's bright red shell, they know to stay away.

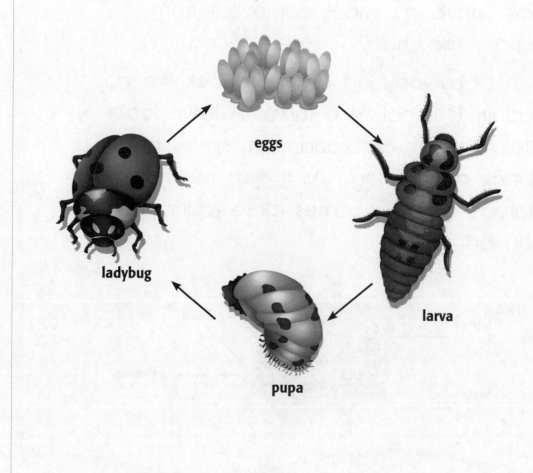

eggs

larva

pupa

ladybug

26

COMMON CORE
STATE STANDARD
W.2.2

Read and analyze the prompt.

Informative/Explanatory Writing Prompt

Compare and contrast an adult ladybug with a larva. How are they alike? How are they different? Use details from the text and the pictures to support your explanation.

Plan the writing.

| Adult Ladybug | Both | Larva |

has two hard red shells on its back with black dots

has a round body

has wings

have six legs

looks like a black caterpillar

has spikes on its back

COMMON CORE
STATE STANDARD
W.2.2

Read and analyze the model.

An Adult Ladybug and a Larva

by Ricky Sanders

In the text "The Lovely Ladybug," it says that an adult ladybug looks very different from a larva.

An adult ladybug has two hard shells on its back. These shells are red with black spots on them. A ladybug hides its wings under these shells when it's not using them. It has a round body. From the picture, you can tell that it has a little head.

A larva, on the other hand, looks more like a caterpillar than a ladybug. From the picture you can tell that it has a dark body with some light spots. It has spikes on its back.

The only way that an adult ladybug and a larva are alike is that they both have six legs. Otherwise, they look completely different.

✔ Writing Checklist: Informative/Explanatory

❏ The writer introduced the topic and responded to the prompt.

❏ The writer used facts from the text.

❏ The writer included a strong ending.

❏ The writer used correct grammar.

❏ The writer used correct capitalization, punctuation, and spelling.

COMMON CORE
STATE STANDARD
W.2.3

Writing a Narrative

Mini-Lesson 5: Respond to Literature

> **COMMON CORE STATE STANDARD W.2.3**
> Write narratives in which they recount two or more appropriately sequenced events, include some details regarding what happened, use temporal words to signal event order, and provide some sense of closure.

Explain to students that they will often encounter narrative writing prompts that instruct them to respond directly to a passage they have read. Tell them that the passage might be fiction. It could be a realistic story, a fantasy, or something that takes place in the past or the future. Then take the following steps to guide students through the process of writing a narrative piece in response to literature.

Read the passage. Distribute pages 31–33 to students. Depending on students' needs, you may wish to read the passage aloud, have students read it with a partner, or have them read it independently.

Read and analyze the prompt. Read the prompt at the top of page 33 with students. Model how to analyze the prompt. Ask questions such as the following:

- *What form of writing does the writing prompt ask for?* (narrative)

- *How can you tell?* (The prompt is asking me to write a sequel to the story "Walking Boomer.")

- *What is the purpose of the assignment?* (to write a new story based on the details in "Walking Boomer")

- *What information do I need to complete the task?* (I need to use details from the story "Walking Boomer" and my imagination.)

Plan the writing. Use page 33 to model how to plan writing a narrative. Draw the graphic organizer on the board. As you fill in the annotations from the student model, discuss why each is appropriate. Allow students to add their own suggestions as well.

Read and analyze the model. Distribute the student writing model and checklist on pages 34–35 to students. Read them aloud. Discuss with students whether or not the writer was successful at accomplishing the task. Ask them to complete the checklist as you discuss the narrative.

Read the passage below.

Walking Boomer

1. It was a beautiful day, so Ava decided to take Boomer, her family's puppy, for a walk. She had just snapped Boomer's leash onto his collar when her friend Liz rang the doorbell.

2. "Hi Liz," Ava said. "Do you want to come for a walk with Boomer and me?"

3. Boomer was very excited to see Liz and jumped up on her and licked her face, which made Liz laugh. "Sure," she said.

4. Ava was surprised at how hard Boomer tugged on his leash. "He's making my arms hurt," she said. Then the problem became worse.

(continued)

Common Core
State Standard
W.2.3

(continued)

5. Boomer spotted another dog a few houses away and tugged on his leash super-hard. Then he slipped out of his collar and ran after the dog.

6. "Boomer!" Ava and Liz shouted, but it was no use. Boomer kept on running.

7. Ava and Liz chased him up the street, but he would not come to them. Then Ava had an idea. She held Boomer's leash high up in the air. "Boomer, do you want to go for a walk?" she asked.

8. It worked! Boomer ran to Ava, and she slipped the collar over his head and tightened it. Liz and Ava laughed all the way home.

Read and analyze the prompt.

Narrative Writing Prompt

Write a new story about the next time
Ava and Liz take Boomer for a walk.
What happens? What do Ava and Liz
do differently this time?

Plan the writing.

Characters:	**Setting:**
Ava, Liz, and the puppy Boomer	outdoors

Events from the Text I Read:
The last time Ava and Liz walked Boomer, he tugged hard on his leash. He made Ava's arms hurt. Then he slipped out of his collar and ran after another dog.

Resolution:
This time, Ava makes sure his collar is on tight, and Ava and Liz both hold onto his leash when he tugs. They tell him "No!" and will not walk if he tugs hard, so Ava's arms won't hurt.

Read and analyze the model.

Walking Boomer—Again

by Julia Harrison

Ava and Liz were getting ready to walk Boomer again. Ava leaned over and checked Boomer's collar. "I want to make sure this is on tight," she said. "I don't want him getting away from us again."

Liz snapped the leash onto Boomer's collar. "Today, Boomer, we're going to teach you not to pull so hard on your leash," she said.

Then they headed outside. This time, Ava and Liz both held onto his leash so that Ava's arms wouldn't hurt.

As soon as he started to pull, though, they stopped walking. "No!" Ava said. "Walk nice, Boomer." Boomer started to walk again—and then he tugged. Ava did this again—and then again. Eventually, Boomer seemed to get it.

Then Boomer saw a dog and tugged really hard. Ava and Liz both tugged back and yelled "No!" Boomer sat down but then he started to whimper. Liz kissed his head and rubbed behind his ears.

By the end of the walk, Boomer still was not perfect, but he was much better at walking on a leash than the last time.

✔ **Writing Checklist: Narrative**

- ❏ The writer gave the title of the story and wrote about one or more events.
- ❏ The writer put the events in an order that made sense.
- ❏ The writer used time words to show the order.
- ❏ The writer included a strong ending.
- ❏ The writer used correct grammar.
- ❏ The writer used correct capitalization, punctuation, and spelling.

COMMON CORE
STATE STANDARD
W.2.3

Writing a Narrative

Mini-Lesson 6: Respond to Informational Text

> **COMMON CORE STATE STANDARD W.2.3**
> Write narratives in which they recount two or more appropriately sequenced events, include some details regarding what happened, use temporal words to signal event order, and provide some sense of closure.

Explain to students that they will often encounter narrative writing prompts that instruct them to respond directly to a passage they have read. Tell them that the passage might be nonfiction. It might be a passage about science or social studies, a how-to passage, a biography or an autobiography, or a digital source. Then take the following steps to guide students through the process of writing a narrative piece in response to an informational text.

Read the passage. Distribute pages 37–39 to students. Depending on students' needs, you may wish to read the passage aloud, have students read it with a partner, or have them read it independently.

Read and analyze the prompt. Read the prompt at the top of page 39 with students. Model how to analyze the prompt. Ask questions such as the following:

- *What form of writing does the writing prompt ask for?* (narrative)

- *How can you tell?* (The prompt is to write a story about someone who lives in a tepee.)

- *What is the purpose of the assignment?* (to write a narrative and support it with details from the text)

- *What information do I need to complete the task?* (I need to use evidence from the text "Tepees" and my own imagination.)

Plan the writing. Use page 39 to model how to plan writing a narrative. Draw the graphic organizer on the board. As you fill in the annotations from the student model, discuss why each is appropriate. Allow students to add their own suggestions as well.

Read and analyze the model. Distribute the student writing model and checklist on pages 40–41 to students. Read them aloud. Discuss with students whether or not the writer was successful at accomplishing the task. Ask them to complete the checklist as you discuss the narrative.

Read the passage below.

Tepees

1.   The Plains Indians were Native Americans who lived in the Great Plains. This is a flat area in the middle of the United States. The Plains Indians lived in special homes called tepees. A tepee was made from buffalo skins wrapped around long poles that were tied together at the top. A tepee was shaped like a triangle or cone.

2.   Tepees were warm in the winter yet cool in the summer. They could be made in different sizes.

3.   Some were small and built for only two or three people. Others were large enough for twenty or thirty people to sleep in comfortably!

(continued)

COMMON CORE
STATE STANDARD
W.2.3

(continued)

4. The biggest advantage to living in a tepee was that it could be moved easily. The Plains Indians moved from place to place to hunt buffalo. A tepee could be quickly taken down and then set up again in a new place.

5. Women and men had specific roles when it came to caring for tepees. Women were in charge of taking down and setting up tepees. They also maintained order inside a tepee.

6. Men were in charge of gathering materials to build tepees. They also decorated the tepees by painting pictures on the outside. If it rained hard, men had to wrap an extra buffalo skin around the outside of a tepee to keep those inside dry.

7. In the winter, the Plains Indians built a fire inside their tepees to cook food and stay warm. Tepees had an open space at the top, so the smoke could escape.

Common Core Writing to Texts Grade 2 • ©2014 Newmark Learning, LLC

Read and analyze the prompt.

Narrative Writing Prompt

Write a story about a boy or girl who is a Plains Indian. Be sure to name your character and tell how his or her family moves to a new place. Use details from the text in your story.

Plan the writing.

Characters:	Setting:
Anna, a young girl, and her mother	Great Plains

Details from the Text I Read:
Tepees are made of buffalo skins. These skins are wrapped around poles tied together at the top. Women were in charge of taking down and setting up tepees when the Plains Indians needed to move to follow the buffalo.

Problem:
Anna does not want to move again. She likes where her tribe is now.

COMMON CORE
STATE STANDARD
W.2.3

Read and analyze the model.

Why Do We Have to Move Again?

by Michelle Ryan

Anna sat inside her family's tepee. She could hear other members of her tribe beginning to pack up their belongings. Some were already taking down their tepees. Anna did not want to move. She liked this area. It was near a pretty creek that was fun to explore. She was tired of traveling.

"Anna," her mother said. "It is almost time to go. Please help me take down our tepee."

Anna folded her arms across her chest. "Why do we have to move again? I don't want to go to a new place. I like it here!"

"You know the answer to that, my daughter. The buffalo herd has moved. If we do not go, we may not have food to eat."

Anna sighed. She knew her mother was right. It was the Plains Indians' way of life to follow the buffalo herd. She rose and helped her mother remove the painted buffalo skin that was the outside of their home. Then they tied the poles together and put the skin and the poles on the back of a large horse. It was time to go again.

Common Core Writing to Texts Grade 2 • ©2014 Newmark Learning, LLC

✓ Writing Checklist: Narrative

❏ The writer gave the title of the story and wrote about one or more events.

❏ The writer put the events in an order that made sense.

❏ The writer used time words to show the order.

❏ The writer included a strong ending.

❏ The writer used correct grammar.

❏ The writer used correct capitalization, punctuation, and spelling.

Practice Texts with Prompts

How to Use Practice Texts with Prompts

This section of *Writing to Texts* provides opportunities for students to practice writing frequently in a wide range of genres and provides authentic practice for standardized writing assessments. Each practice lesson contains a passage followed by three prompts. Below each prompt is a graphic organizer to help students plan their writing.

Before beginning, assign students one of the prompts, or ask them each to choose one. Explain to students that they are to plan and write an essay about the passage or passages according to the instructions in the chosen prompt. They should write on a separate piece of paper, or in a writing journal designated for writing practice.

There are various ways to use the practice section. You may wish to have students complete the writing tasks at independent workstations, as homework assignments, or as test practice in a timed environment.

If you choose to use these as practice for standardized tests, assign one prompt and give students 60 minutes to execute the task. In using these as test practice, tell students that they should think of their writing as a draft, and tell them they will not have additional time to revise their work.

You may also choose to have students respond to the prompts orally to strengthen academic oral language skills.

On pages 124–125, reproducible Student Writing Checklists are provided. Distribute them to students to serve as checklists as they write, or as self-assessment guides.

Conducting Research

The Common Core State Standards require that students are provided opportunities to learn research techniques and to apply these skills in their preparation of projects. The passages in this section can make for research project starters. After students respond to an informational prompt, ask them to conduct further research on information from the practice text in order to build their knowledge.

Explain to students that researchers take good notes, connect new knowledge to what is already known, organize information into sensible layouts for a report, cite their sources, and use their own words to convey the information.

Tell students to gather information from print and digital sources. Have them take brief notes on sources and sort their facts, details, and evidence into categories.

Practice Texts with Prompts Table of Contents

COMMON CORE
STATE STANDARDS
W.2.1–
W.2.8

Name_____ Date_____

Read the passage below.

The Talent Show

1.   Yesterday, I kept sneezing and coughing. "I think I'm getting sick," I told Josh.

2.   "No way!" Josh exclaimed. "Tonight's the talent show. What about our act?"

3.   Josh, Maria, and I were going to do a magic act. I told Josh not to worry. I would be there no matter what.

4.   My mother had other ideas. "Let me feel your forehead, Carlos," she said when she heard me coughing after school.

5.   "I'm fine, Madre. No worries," I said, but she felt my forehead anyway.

6.   Of course I was burning up. She told me to call Josh and tell him that they would have to do the act without me.

7.   I was so disappointed that I wanted to cry. My spirits lifted later. Maria and Josh stopped by after the talent show. Maria had her dad record the entire show. We all watched it together.

Name_____ Date_____

 Opinion/Argument Writing Prompt

Do you think Carlos, Josh, and Maria are good friends to one another? Why or why not? Support your opinion with reasons from the text.

My Opinion:

My Reasons:

1.

2.

3.

COMMON CORE
STATE STANDARDS
**W.2.1–
W.2.8**

Name_____ Date_____

 Informative/Explanatory Writing Prompt

What do Carlos's friends do at the end of the story? Explain how this makes him feel. Use details from the story.

Cause:

Effect:

Name_____ Date_____

COMMON CORE
STATE STANDARDS
W.2.1–
W.2.8

Narrative Writing Prompt

Write a story that includes what Josh and Maria might say to Carlos after they watch the recording of the talent show. Use details from the story in your new story.

Josh:

_____

_____

Maria:

_____

_____

Josh:

_____

_____

Maria:

_____

_____

COMMON CORE
STATE STANDARDS
W.2.1–
W.2.8

Name_____ Date_____

Read the passage below.

Emily's Test

1.   Emily was supposed to go to the castle to see the queen. Her mother had told her to simply follow the golden path. But following the path was not simple.

2.   It divided into two paths, and then three. It did this again and again. Emily did her best to choose the right path. But now she was lost in the forest.

3.   Emily sat down on a rock to eat the sandwich her mother had packed for her. Suddenly, she saw a strange, ugly toad.

4.   "Would you mind sharing your lunch with me?" asked the toad. "I haven't had anything to eat in a long time."

5.   "Here," Emily said, and she gave the toad her sandwich. The toad turned into a fairy.

6.   "Emily, you passed my test," the fairy said. "You are a kind girl. Take my hand, and I will take you to the queen."

7.   Emily took the fairy's hand. They flew into the air and soon arrived at the castle.

48

Name_____ Date_____

COMMON CORE
STATE STANDARDS
W.2.1–
W.2.8

Opinion/Argument Writing Prompt

Was it a good idea for Emily to share her sandwich with a strange toad? Why or why not? Support your opinion with evidence from the story.

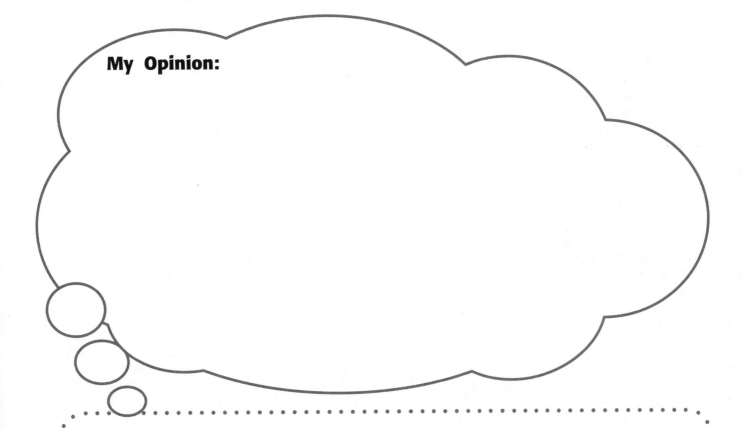

My Opinion:

My Reasons:

COMMON CORE
STATE STANDARDS
**W.2.1–
W.2.8**

Name_____ Date_____

Informative/Explanatory Writing Prompt

Explain what caused Emily to become lost. Use details from the story in your explanation.

Cause:

_____

_____

_____

_____

Effect:

Emily became lost in the forest.

Name_____ Date_____

COMMON CORE
STATE STANDARDS
W.2.1–
W.2.8

 Narrative Writing Prompt

> Rewrite the story from the point of view of the toad. Use words such as *I* and *me* to describe what happens and how the toad feels.

Beginning:

_____

_____

Middle:

_____

_____

End:

_____

_____

COMMON CORE
STATE STANDARDS
W.2.1–
W.2.8

Name_____ Date_____

Read the passage below.

Furless Friends

1.   "Remember, nothing with fur," Kate's mother said, and Kate rolled her eyes. She had heard this many times before. Kate was allergic to animals with fur. When she was around a dog or a cat, she sneezed, and her eyes became sore and itchy.

2.   In spite of her allergies, Kate loved animals, and she desperately wanted a pet. So she and her mother had gone to the pet store.

3.   Kate looked at the fish, but she thought a fish might be boring. Then, she looked at a turtle. Kate liked the turtle, but she was worried the tank might smell. Next, Kate looked at some parakeets. They were cute. Kate thought a parakeet would make a great pet. A saleswoman said that parakeets like the company of other parakeets, so they really should buy two.

4.   "Can we?" Kate asked her mother hopefully.

Common Core Writing to Texts Grade 2 • ©2014 Newmark Learning, LLC

Name_____ Date_____

COMMON CORE
STATE STANDARDS
W.2.1–
W.2.8

 Opinion/Argument Writing Prompt

Do you think Kate made a good decision? Support your opinion with details from the text.

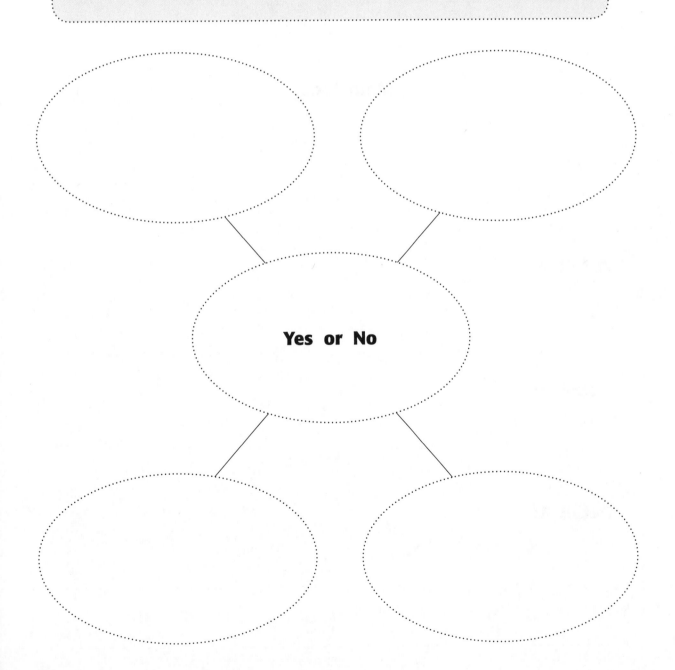

Yes or No

COMMON CORE
STATE STANDARDS
**W.2.1–
W.2.8**

Name_____ Date_____

Informative/Explanatory Writing Prompt

What happens to Kate if she is around a pet with fur? Use details from "Furless Friends" to support your explanation.

Main Idea:
Detail 1:
Detail 2:
Detail 3:

Name_____ Date_____

Narrative Writing Prompt

Write an ending to the story. Imagine what Kate's mother says and what happens next. Include details from "Furless Friends" in your ending.

Beginning:

Middle:

End:

COMMON CORE
STATE STANDARDS
W.2.1–
W.2.8

Name_____ Date_____

Read the passage below.

The Shoemaker and the Elves

1. Once upon a time, there lived a poor shoemaker and his wife. The shoemaker worked very hard, and he was always honest with his customers. He sometimes gave away shoes to people who needed them. But he still could not earn enough money for his own family.

2. One night the shoemaker cut out pieces of leather. He planned to sew them into shoes in the morning. When he awoke, however, the shoes were already made! His customers offered to pay him extra for the shoes.

3. The next night, the shoemaker once again cut out pieces of leather. And when he woke, they were once again sewn into shoes.

4. He and his wife decided to stay up at night to see who was making the shoes. They discovered several elves hard at work!

5. As a thank-you, the shoemaker asked his wife to make them new clothes. The elves did not return after this, but they promised the shoemaker good fortune in the future.

Name_____ Date_____

COMMON CORE
STATE STANDARDS
W.2.1–
W.2.8

 Opinion/Argument Writing Prompt

Why do you think the elves helped the shoemaker? Support your opinion with details from the story.

My Opinion:

Detail:
_____
_____
_____
_____
_____
_____

Detail:
_____
_____
_____
_____
_____
_____

Detail:
_____
_____
_____
_____
_____
_____

COMMON CORE
STATE STANDARDS
W.2.1–
W.2.8

Name_____ Date_____

Informative/Explanatory Writing Prompt

What words can you use to describe the shoemaker? Use details from the text to support your explanation.

Word:

_____

_____

Word:

_____

_____

Shoemaker

Word:

_____

_____

Word:

_____

_____

Common Core Writing to Texts Grade 2 • ©2014 Newmark Learning, LLC

Name_____ Date_____

Narrative Writing Prompt

Write another story in which the elves in "The Shoemaker and the Elves" help someone. Be sure your story has a beginning, a middle, and an ending.

Beginning:

Middle:

End:

COMMON CORE
STATE STANDARDS
W.2.1–
W.2.8

Name_____ Date_____

Read the passage below.

Damon's Problem

1. Damon could not believe it when his friend Jimmy said that he was having a pool party for his birthday.

2. "That's going to be amazing," he said as he faked a smile. Damon had a big problem: He did not know how to swim.

3. Damon told his older brother Raymond about his problem. Raymond laughed.

4. "It's not funny!" Damon yelled. "I can't go to Jimmy's party if I can't swim."

5. Raymond said he would help. Each day after school, he took Damon to the pool at the community center. He held him up and taught him the right way to kick. He showed him how to move his arms.

6. Before Damon knew it, he could swim from one end of the pool to the other. Now he couldn't wait to go to Jimmy's birthday party.

Common Core Writing to Texts Grade 2 • ©2014 Newmark Learning, LLC

Name_____ Date_____

COMMON CORE
STATE STANDARDS
W.2.1–
W.2.8

 Opinion/Argument Writing Prompt

Do you think a swimming pool is a good place for a birthday party? Why or why not? Support your opinion with evidence from "Damon's Problem."

My Opinion:

Detail 1:

Detail 2:

Detail 3:

Closing Sentence:

COMMON CORE
STATE STANDARDS
W.2.1–
W.2.8

Name_____ Date_____

 Informative/Explanatory Writing Prompt

How did Raymond teach Damon to swim? Use details from the text to support your explanation.

Order of Events
1.
2.
3.
4.

Name_____ Date_____

COMMON CORE
STATE STANDARDS
W.2.1–
W.2.8

 Narrative Writing Prompt

In this story, Raymond helps Damon. Write a sequel in which Damon helps Raymond. What will Raymond's problem be? How will Damon help him solve it?

Problem:

Solution:

COMMON CORE
STATE STANDARDS
**W.2.1–
W.2.8**

Name_____ Date_____

Read the passage below.

The Rain Forest

1. When I walked into my classroom on the first day of second grade, a teacher I did not know was in the room. I though that Ms. Reed would be my teacher! I had looked forward to having her as my teacher.

2. The woman, Mrs. Cooper, told us that Ms. Reed had moved. Mrs. Cooper said that she would be our teacher. I was upset.

3. Then Mrs. Cooper told us that she was a teacher, but she was also an artist. She said that we would be studying the rain forest this year. She said that she thought it would be fun to turn our classroom into a rain forest!

4. "We'll cover the walls with green tissue paper," she said. "We'll cover the ceiling and the walls with vines. We'll make large rain forest animals out of cardboard and paint them."

5. As I listened to her plans, I thought maybe having Mrs. Cooper as a teacher wouldn't be so bad after all!

Common Core Writing to Texts Grade 2 • ©2014 Newmark Learning, LLC

COMMON CORE
STATE STANDARDS
**W.2.1–
W.2.8**

Name_____ Date_____

Opinion/Argument Writing Prompt

If you were a student in Mrs. Cooper's class, would you like the idea of turning your classroom into a rain forest? Why or why not? Support your opinion with details from the story.

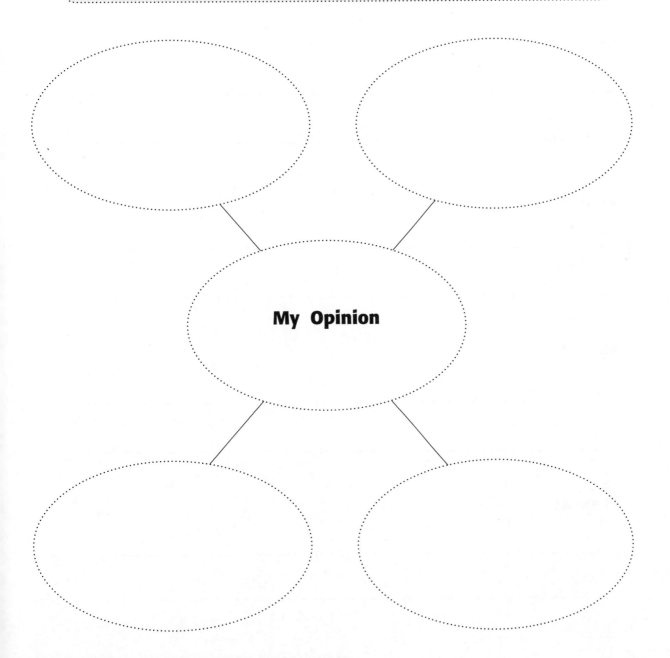

My Opinion

COMMON CORE
STATE STANDARDS
W.2.1–
W.2.8

Name_____ Date_____

Informative/Explanatory Writing Prompt

How do you turn a classroom into a rain forest? Support your explanation with details from the text.

Step 1:
_____
_____

Step 2:
_____
_____

Step 3:
_____
_____

Step 4:
_____
_____

Common Core Writing to Texts Grade 2 • ©2014 Newmark Learning, LLC

Name_____ Date_____

Narrative Writing Prompt

Write a journal entry that the narrator might record after her first week of school in the second grade. Use information from "The Rain Forest."

First:

Next:

Last:

COMMON CORE
STATE STANDARDS
W.2.1–
W.2.8

Name_____ Date_____

Read the passage below.

The Lucky Charm

1. Amelia was having a great month. She was doing well in school and even won an art contest. Her mother had agreed to let her have a sleepover. Amelia took her charm out of her pocket. She thought it brought her luck. *This is why so many good things are happening*, she thought.

2. Amelia had a test the next week. She had spent many hours studying and was certain that she would do well. Then the morning of the test, Amelia could not find her lucky charm anywhere. She told Ms. Gonzales, her teacher, about her problem.

3. "Did you study for this test?" her teacher asked. Amelia said that she had studied very hard. "Then you will do well."

4. Ms. Gonzales smiled at Amelia when she collected Amelia's test. "Did you do well?"

5. "I'm sure I did," Amelia replied.

6. "See? There is no need for a lucky charm, just hard work," explained her teacher.

Common Core Writing to Texts Grade 2 • ©2014 Newmark Learning, LLC

Name_____ Date_____

Opinion/Argument Writing Prompt

At the end of the first paragraph, Amelia thinks that good things have happened to her because of her good luck charm. Do you think this is true? Explain why or why not. Use details from the story.

My Opinion:

My Reasons:

1.

2.

3.

COMMON CORE
STATE STANDARDS
**W.2.1–
W.2.8**

Name_____ Date_____

Informative/Explanatory Writing Prompt

What can you tell about Ms. Gonzales from the story "The Lucky Charm"? Use details from the story to support your explanation.

What Ms. Gonzales Says:	**What Ms. Gonzales Does:**
_____	_____
_____	_____
_____	_____
_____	_____
_____	_____
_____	_____
_____	_____
_____	_____

Common Core Writing to Texts Grade 2 • ©2014 Newmark Learning, LLC

Name_____ Date_____

COMMON CORE
STATE STANDARDS
**W.2.1–
W.2.8**

 Narrative Writing Prompt

Write a story about what happens when Amelia gets home from school. Have her talk to her mother about how she did on her test.

Amelia:

_____

_____

Mom:

_____

_____

Amelia:

_____

_____

Mom:

_____

_____

COMMON CORE
STATE STANDARDS
W.2.1–
W.2.8

Name_____ Date_____

Read the passage below.

Why the Sky Is High

1. A long time ago, the sky was very low. People could not even stand up straight. If they did, they would touch the sky.

2. The people back then lived in small mud huts. One summer it was very hot and dry. Then the mud huts became very dusty.

3. The dust was everywhere. It was on the trees. It covered people's yards and sidewalks. It covered the roofs of their mud huts. The dust made it hard for people to breathe and see. It made them sneeze.

4. The people kept trying to sweep the dust away from their huts. When they swept, however, they pushed the dust into the air.

5. The sky did not like so much dust. He could not breathe. It made him sneeze again and again. He could not stand it any longer, so he moved up high away from the people. This is why the sky is high.

COMMON CORE
STATE STANDARDS
**W.2.1–
W.2.8**

Name_____ Date_____

Opinion/Argument Writing Prompt

Why do you think the tale "Why the Sky Is High" was originally told? State your opinion and use evidence from the tale to support your argument.

My Opinion:

_____

_____

_____

My Reasons:

_____

_____

_____

_____

_____

_____

COMMON CORE
STATE STANDARDS
W.2.1–
W.2.8

Name_____ Date_____

Informative/Explanatory Writing Prompt

What made the sky move up high and away from the village? Support your explanation with details from the story.

Main Idea:
Detail 1:
Detail 2:
Detail 3:

Common Core Writing to Texts Grade 2 • ©2014 Newmark Learning, LLC

Name_____ Date_____

COMMON CORE
STATE STANDARDS
**W.2.1–
W.2.8**

 Narrative Writing Prompt

Rewrite the story from the sky's point of view. Use words such as *I* and *me* to describe what happens and how you feel.

Beginning:

_____

_____

Middle:

_____

_____

End:

_____

_____

COMMON CORE
STATE STANDARDS
W.2.1–
W.2.8

Name_____ Date_____

Read the passage below.

At the Zoo

1. My grandma took me to the zoo
2. For my own special day.
3. It was my seventh birthday
4. And a sunny day in May.

5. I saw a silly monkey
6. That was climbing up a tree.
7. His tail held on just like a hand
8. And then he waved at me.

9. Next we saw the elephants,
10. A mommy and a baby.
11. I'd like to take them home with me,
12. And Grandma did say maybe.

13. My favorite was the tiger
14. With his loud "good morning" roar.
15. Shiny black and orange stripes
16. Is what the tiger wore.

17. We walked out through the gift shop
18. and Grandma said, "Pick one."
19. I picked a book of animals
20. To remind us of our fun.

Common Core Writing to Texts Grade 2 • ©2014 Newmark Learning, LLC

Name_____ Date_____

COMMON CORE
STATE STANDARDS
W.2.1–
W.2.8

 Opinion/Argument Writing Prompt

Do you think a zoo is a good place for a grandmother to take a seven-year-old child? Why or why not? Support your opinion with details from the poem.

My Opinion:

Detail 1:

Detail 2:

Detail 3:

Closing Sentence:

COMMON CORE
STATE STANDARDS
W.2.1–
W.2.8

Name_____ Date_____

 Informative/Explanatory Writing Prompt

The speaker of "At the Zoo" sees a tiger.
What does this tiger look and sound like?
Use details from the poem to support
your explanation.

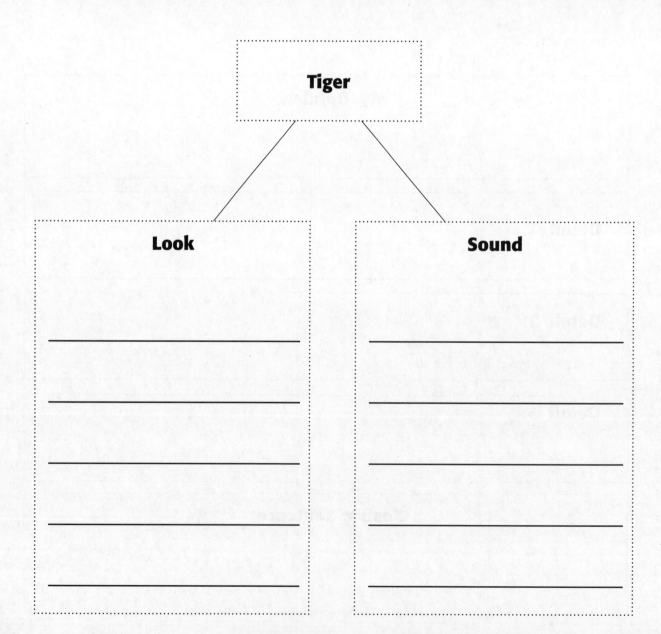

Tiger

Look

_____

_____

_____

_____

_____

Sound

_____

_____

_____

_____

_____

78

Name_____ Date_____

COMMON CORE
STATE STANDARDS
**W.2.1–
W.2.8**

Narrative Writing Prompt

Rewrite the poem as a story. Give the speaker of the poem a name and tell what happens when Grandma takes her to the zoo.

1:
_____

2:
_____

3:
_____

4:
_____

5:
_____

COMMON CORE
STATE STANDARDS
W.2.1–
W.2.8

Name_____ Date_____

Read the passage below.

The Cat Who Walked by Himself

1. *(Cat, Dog, and Cow look at a house.)*

2. **DOG:** I am so cold and hungry. I bet Man and Woman are warm by the fire. I bet they even have food to eat. I'm going to ask them if I can live in that house.

3. **CAT:** I would never give up my freedom to live in a house! I walk by myself.

4. *(Dog barks at the door.)*

5. **WOMAN:** You can live with us if you guard our house.

6. **COW:** I'm cold and hungry. I am going to see if Woman and Man will take me in.

7. *(Cow moos at the door.)*

8. **MAN:** You can live with us if you give us milk.

9. **CAT:** What fools! My freedom is worth more than food and shelter!

10. *(Cold winds blow. Cat shivers and is hungry. She goes to the house.)*

11. **WOMAN:** You can live with us if you chase away the mice.

12. *(Cat purrs and agrees.)*

 Common Core Writing to Texts Grade 2 • ©2014 Newmark Learning, LLC

Name_____ Date_____

 Opinion/Argument Writing Prompt

Imagine that you are an animal. Do you think it is better to be free or to live with people? Use details from the play to support your opinion.

My Opinion:

My Reasons:

1.

2.

3.

COMMON CORE
STATE STANDARDS
W.2.1–
W.2.8

Name_____ Date_____

 Informative/Explanatory Writing Prompt

What makes Cat change her mind and go to the house? Use details from the play to support your explanation.

Cause:

Effect:

Common Core Writing to Texts Grade 2 • ©2014 Newmark Learning, LLC

Name_____ Date_____

COMMON CORE
STATE STANDARDS
**W.2.1–
W.2.8**

Narrative Writing Prompt

Rewrite the play as a story told from Cat's point of view. Use words such as *I* and *me* to describe what happens and how you feel.

Beginning:

Middle:

End:

COMMON CORE
STATE STANDARDS
W.2.1–
W.2.8

Name_____ Date_____

Read the passage below.

Tree Rings

1.   Trees are plants. Like other plants, trees have a stem. The stem of a tree is a trunk. The trunk is covered with a rough coat of bark. Under the bark are more layers, or coats, of wood.

2.   A tree grows one layer of new wood each year. These layers are called "tree rings," and they can be seen after the tree has been cut into logs.

3.   Each end of a log looks like a big circle. Many tree rings can be seen inside this circle. Each tree ring has a light-colored part and a dark-colored part. The light-colored part is wood that 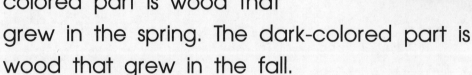 grew in the spring. The dark-colored part is wood that grew in the fall.

4.   The largest rings found just under the bark are the newest layers of wood. The smallest rings near the center of the circle are the oldest layers. By counting all the rings, people can tell the age of a tree.

 Common Core Writing to Texts Grade 2 • ©2014 Newmark Learning, LLC

Name_____ Date_____

COMMON CORE
STATE STANDARDS
W.2.1–
W.2.8

Opinion/Argument Writing Prompt

Suppose your science teacher asked you to give a presentation. Do you think tree rings would be a good topic for your presentation? Why or why not? Support your opinion with details from the text.

My Opinion:

My Reasons:

1.

2.

3.

COMMON CORE
STATE STANDARDS
W.2.1–
W.2.8

Name_____ Date_____

Informative/Explanatory Writing Prompt

A friend has a log and wants to know how old the tree was. Explain to her how to find the age of the tree. Use details from the passage to support your explanation.

Main Idea:

Detail 1:

Detail 2:

Detail 3:

Name_____ Date_____

COMMON CORE
STATE STANDARDS
W.2.1–
W.2.8

 Narrative Writing Prompt

Write a narrative story in which a character who is your age learns how to tell how old a tree is from looking at the rings of a log. Be sure to include a beginning, a middle, and an end.

Beginning:

Middle:

End:

COMMON CORE
STATE STANDARDS
W.2.1–
W.2.8

Name_____ Date_____

Read the passage below.

The United States: A Melting Pot

1. When people make soup, they put many different foods into one pot. Each food has its own flavor, or taste. As the soup cooks, these tastes all mix together. Soon everything just starts to taste like soup. The United States is much like a pot of soup.

2. A long time ago, immigrants started moving to the United States. Immigrants are people who leave one country to live in another.

3. Immigrants came to the United States from all different countries. At times, thousands of immigrants entered the country each day. Each group of immigrants had its own way of life. They spoke different languages.

4. But the longer different groups lived near one another, the more their ways of life began to mix together.

5. The many small groups had mixed together to form one big group of Americans: a "melting pot."

Name_____ Date_____

COMMON CORE
STATE STANDARDS
**W.2.1–
W.2.8**

 Opinion/Argument Writing Prompt

Do you think calling the United States a "melting pot" makes sense? Support your opinion with reasons from the text.

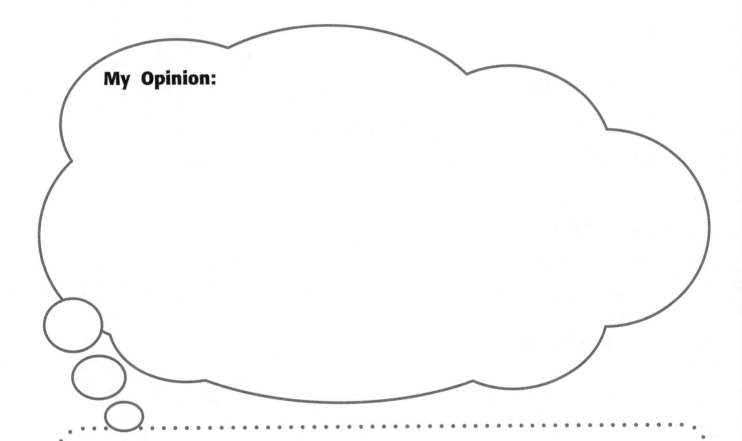

My Opinion:

My Reasons:

Common Core
State Standards
W.2.1–
W.2.8

Name_____ Date_____

 Informative/Explanatory Writing Prompt

Explain what happened when immigrants came to the United States from other countries. Use details from the text and your own ideas to support your explanation.

Main Idea:
Reason 1:
Reason 2:
Reason 3:

Name_____ Date_____

 Narrative Writing Prompt

Write a story called "The Melting Pot."
Have it take place in a neighborhood
where immigrants from many different
countries live. Use details from the text
in your story.

Beginning:

_____

_____

Middle:

_____

_____

End:

_____

_____

COMMON CORE
STATE STANDARDS
**W.2.1–
W.2.8**

Name_____ Date_____

Read the passage below.

George Washington Carver

1. George Washington Carver was an important inventor. He discovered more than 300 ways to use peanuts.

2. George was born on a small farm in Missouri in 1864. His mother was a slave. When slavery ended, George wanted to go to school.

3. George was very smart. But back then, it wasn't easy for African Americans to go to school. Most schools were only for white students. George had to travel far to go to school. He studied hard for years.

4. George learned a great deal about plants. At the time, most farmers in the South grew cotton. George taught them that growing just one crop harms the soil. George wanted them to grow peanuts too. But the farmers worried that no one would buy all the peanuts.

5. So George invented many new ways to use peanuts. For example, he used peanuts to make cooking oil and fuel for automobiles—and of course, peanut butter.

Name_____ Date_____

COMMON CORE
STATE STANDARDS
**W.2.1–
W.2.8**

 Opinion/Argument Writing Prompt

Do you think it's important for people to invent new things? Why or why not? Support your opinion with details from the text.

My Opinion:

Detail 1:

Detail 2:

Detail 3:

Closing Sentence:

COMMON CORE
STATE STANDARDS
**W.2.1–
W.2.8**

Name_____ Date_____

Informative/Explanatory Writing Prompt

What can you tell about George Washington Carver from the text? What kind of person was he? Support your explanation with details from the text.

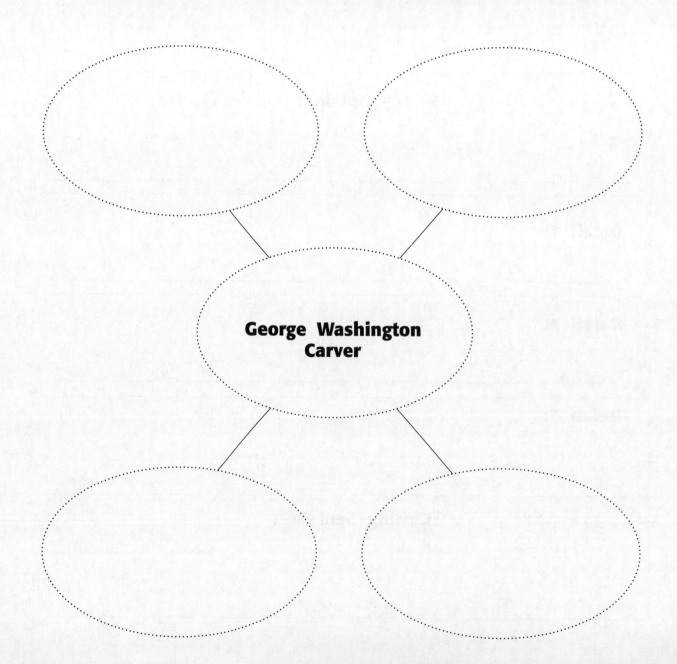

George Washington Carver

Name_____ Date_____

COMMON CORE
STATE STANDARDS
**W.2.1–
W.2.8**

Narrative Writing Prompt

Write a conversation between George and a farmer who grows only cotton. The farmer should explain to George that his cotton is not growing as well as it used to.

Farmer:

_____

_____

George:

_____

_____

Farmer:

_____

_____

George:

_____

_____

COMMON CORE
STATE STANDARDS
W.2.1–
W.2.8

Name_____ Date_____

Read the passage below.

How to Grow Sunflowers

1.   A sunflower has a very tall stem and a bright yellow blossom, or flower. Sunflowers can grow to be 12 feet (3.7 meters) tall! Many people like to grow sunflowers because they are big and beautiful. People also like to roast and eat the seeds in the flower part of the plant. Sunflowers are easy to grow if you follow these steps:

2.   **Step 1:** Buy some sunflower seeds. Most discount stores sell sunflower seeds.

3.   **Step 2:** In the spring, find a sunny place in a yard or garden.

4.   **Step 3:** Plant the seeds in the soil. Push them about 2 inches (5.1 centimeters) into the ground. Plant seeds about 3 feet (0.9 meter) apart.

5.   **Step 4:** Water the seeds a little bit every day unless it rains.

6.   **Step 5:** Once the sunflowers are about 1 foot (0.3 meter) tall, tie each of them to a stick. This keeps the sunflower plant from bending over as the flower grows and becomes heavy.

Name_____ Date_____

Opinion/Argument Writing Prompt

Why do you think many people like to grow sunflowers? Support your opinion with details from the text.

My Opinion:

My Reasons:

1.

2.

3.

COMMON CORE
STATE STANDARDS
W.2.1–
W.2.8

Name_____ Date_____

Informative/Explanatory Writing Prompt

Explain how to grow a sunflower. Use details from the text to support your explanation.

Step 1:
Step 2:
Step 3:
Step 4:
Step 5:

Common Core Writing to Texts Grade 2 • ©2014 Newmark Learning, LLC

Name_____ Date_____

Narrative Writing Prompt

Write a story about someone your age who grows sunflowers for the first time. Be sure your story has a beginning, a middle, and an end. Use details from the text in your story.

Beginning:

Middle:

End:

COMMON CORE
STATE STANDARDS
W.2.1–
W.2.8

Name_____ Date_____

Read the passage below.

Koko the Gorilla

1. Koko the gorilla was born in the San Francisco Zoo in 1971. She is the first gorilla to have learned sign language.

2. Sign language is a way of communicating without words. People who "talk" this way make letters and words with their hands.

3. Koko has learned more than 1,000 signs. She can also understand about 2,000 spoken words. She can tell her caregivers if she is hungry or wants a doll to play with. She can use sign language to ask them questions about visitors.

4. From Koko, scientists have learned that some animals can communicate. They have learned that these animals can think and have emotions like people. Koko has told her caregivers that she would like to have a baby, and if she does, she would teach it sign language as well.

Common Core Writing to Texts Grade 2 • ©2014 Newmark Learning, LLC

Name_____ Date_____

 Opinion/Argument Writing Prompt

Do you think it is important for scientists to study animals such as gorillas? Why or why not? Use details from the text and your own ideas to support your opinion.

My Opinion:

Reason 1:

Reason 2:

Reason 3:

COMMON CORE
STATE STANDARDS
W.2.1–
W.2.8

Name_____ Date_____

Informative/Explanatory Writing Prompt

What have scientists learned from Koko the gorilla? Use details from the text to support your explanation.

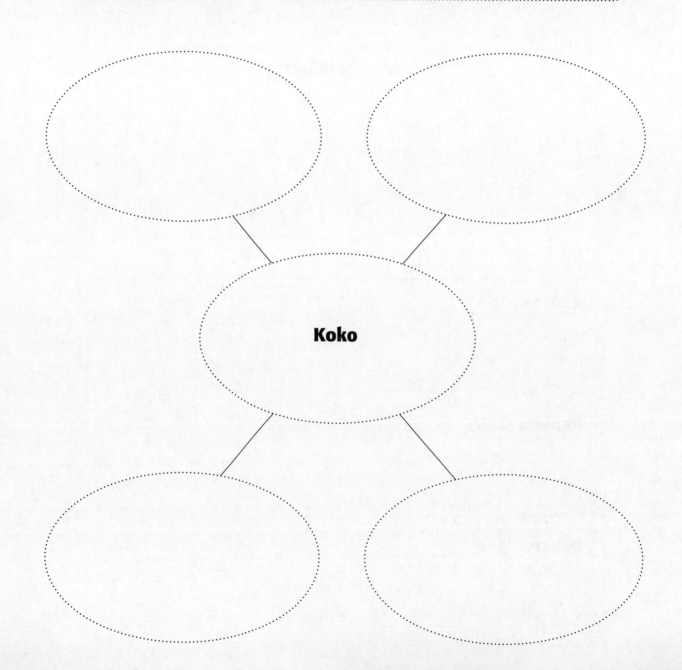

Koko

Name_____ Date_____

COMMON CORE
STATE STANDARDS
**W.2.1–
W.2.8**

 Narrative Writing Prompt

Imagine that you have met Koko. Write a story telling about the experience. Use words such as *I* and *me* to describe what happens and how you feel.

Beginning:

Middle:

End:

COMMON CORE
STATE STANDARDS
W.2.1–
W.2.8

Name_____ Date_____

Read the passage below.

Early Types of Money

1. People did not always use coins and paper money. Thousands of years ago, people bartered, or traded, for what they needed.

2. This did not always work. Suppose a farmer grew corn and wanted to trade his corn for things he needed. What if no one wanted the farmer's corn? Then the farmer wouldn't be able to get what he needed.

3. Long ago, people in China, Africa, and other places began using seashells as money. However, there was a problem with using shells as money. People who lived near the ocean were much richer than those who did not.

4. This changed when countries formed governments. In time, governments set standards for money. For example, a ten-dollar bill might have represented a certain amount of gold or other valuables. This standardizing of money led to the coins and paper money we use today.

Name_____ Date_____

COMMON CORE
STATE STANDARDS
W.2.1–
W.2.8

 Opinion/Argument Writing Prompt

Do you think a standard money system is a good idea? Why or why not? Support your opinion with details from the text.

My Opinion:
Detail 1:
Detail 2:
Detail 3:
Closing Sentence:

COMMON CORE
STATE STANDARDS
W.2.1–
W.2.8

Name_____ Date_____

 Informative/Explanatory Writing Prompt

Why has the type of money people use changed over the years? Use details from the text to support your explanation.

Main Idea:
Detail 1:
Detail 2:
Detail 3:

Name_____ Date_____

COMMON CORE
STATE STANDARDS
**W.2.1–
W.2.8**

 Narrative Writing Prompt

Write a story about a farmer who wants to trade corn for something he needs. Imagine that this farmer has a problem when he tries to do this. Tell how the farmer solves his problem.

Characters:

Setting:

Problem:

How the Problem Is Solved:

COMMON CORE
STATE STANDARDS
W.2.1–
W.2.8

Name_____ Date_____

Read the passage below.

Healthy Eating

1.   Eating nutritious foods gives kids more energy and even helps them to do better in school! Children should eat protein, fruits, vegetables, grains, and dairy products each day.

2.   Protein helps keep muscles and bones strong. Foods that are high in protein come from animals and plants. Fish, chicken, lean meat, eggs, nuts, beans, and peas are good sources of protein.

3.   Fruit and vegetables contain many important vitamins that help heal cuts and keep teeth and gums healthy. They help prevent sickness and disease.

4.   Whole grains contain fiber, which helps move food through the body and prevents disease. Sources of whole grains include whole wheat bread, oatmeal, and brown rice.

5.   The calcium in milk keeps bones strong. Calcium is also in yogurt and cheese.

Common Core Writing to Texts Grade 2 • ©2014 Newmark Learning, LLC

Name_____ Date_____

Opinion/Argument Writing Prompt

Do you think good nutrition is important? Why or why not? Support your opinion with details from the text.

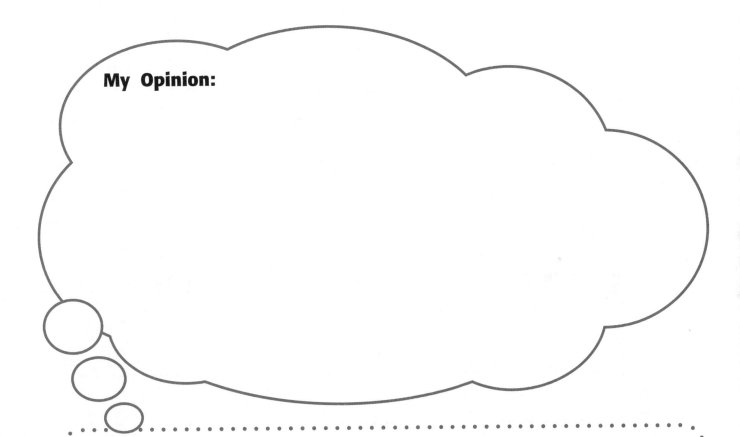

My Opinion:

My Reasons:

COMMON CORE
STATE STANDARDS
W.2.1–
W.2.8

Name_____ Date_____

Informative/Explanatory Writing Prompt

Why is it important to eat protein, fruit, and vegetables? Use details from the text to support your explanation.

Main Idea:		
Reason:	**Reason:**	**Reason:**
_____	_____	_____
_____	_____	_____
_____	_____	_____
_____	_____	_____
_____	_____	_____

Name_____ Date_____

COMMON CORE
STATE STANDARDS
**W.2.1–
W.2.8**

Narrative Writing Prompt

Write a story about a kid who does not eat nutritious foods at first, but learns to change his or her eating habits. Use details from the text in your story.

Characters:

Setting:

Problem:

How the Problem Is Solved:

COMMON CORE
STATE STANDARDS
W.2.1–
W.2.8

Name_____ Date_____

Read the passage below.

Desert Geography

1.   A desert is a place that is very dry. A desert gets less than ten inches of rain per year. There are both hot and cold deserts. The Sahara Desert in Africa is the largest hot desert. The Antarctic Desert is the largest cold desert.

2.   The Sahara Desert in North Africa is almost as big as the entire United States. It is extremely hot and dry. Strong winds blow sand there, creating tall sand dunes. Large rocks and mountains can also be found there. Many plants and animals live in this desert. However, few people call the Sahara Desert home.

3.   The Antarctic Desert in Antarctica is covered in ice. It is located at the South Pole. The coldest temperature on Earth was recorded there: –130°F (–90°C). It is too cold in the Antarctic Desert for people to live there. Trees, bushes, and grass do not grow there. Animals live only in the nearby ocean.

Name_____ Date_____

COMMON CORE
STATE STANDARDS
W.2.1–
W.2.8

Opinion/Argument Writing Prompt

Which would you rather learn more about, the Sahara Desert or the Antarctic Desert? Why? Support your opinion with details from the text.

My Opinion:

Reason:	Reason:	Reason:
_____	_____	_____
_____	_____	_____
_____	_____	_____
_____	_____	_____

COMMON CORE
STATE STANDARDS
W.2.1–
W.2.8

Name_____ Date_____

 Informative/Explanatory Writing Prompt

Explain why people do not live in the Antarctic Desert. Use details from the text to support your explanation.

Main Idea:
Reason 1:
Reason 2:
Reason 3:

Name_____ Date_____

COMMON CORE
STATE STANDARDS
W.2.1–
W.2.8

Narrative Writing Prompt

Write a story from the point of view of someone who visits the Sahara Desert. Be sure to name your character and tell what he or she does and sees. Use details from the story.

First:

Next:

Then:

Last:

COMMON CORE
STATE STANDARDS
W.2.1–
W.2.8

Name_____ Date_____

Read the passage below.

The Daily News

FEBRUARY 28

Cupcake's Amazing Trip
by Rita Santos

1. Boca Raton, Florida—

2. "It's truly a miracle," said Marian Price as she held her cat Cupcake in her arms. Cupcake's amazing journey has made her famous. It all began with a camping trip in a mobile home. Two months ago, Marian and her husband, Dan, were staying at a campground about 150 miles from their home. Cupcake was with them, but she escaped during the night.

3. "We still hoped that someone would find her and call us, but we had to leave because Dan and I had to go back to work," Marian said with tears in her eyes.

4. Then, two months later, Dan heard a faint meow in their backyard. They were amazed to see Cupcake come out of the bushes.

5. The little cat had walked 150 miles home. "She was skinny, dirty, and exhausted but otherwise okay," said Marian.

Common Core Writing to Texts Grade 2 • ©2014 Newmark Learning, LLC

Name_____ Date_____

COMMON CORE
STATE STANDARDS
**W.2.1–
W.2.8**

Opinion/Argument Writing Prompt

Do you think "Cupcake's Amazing Trip" is a good story to print in a newspaper? Why or why not? Support your opinion with details from the text.

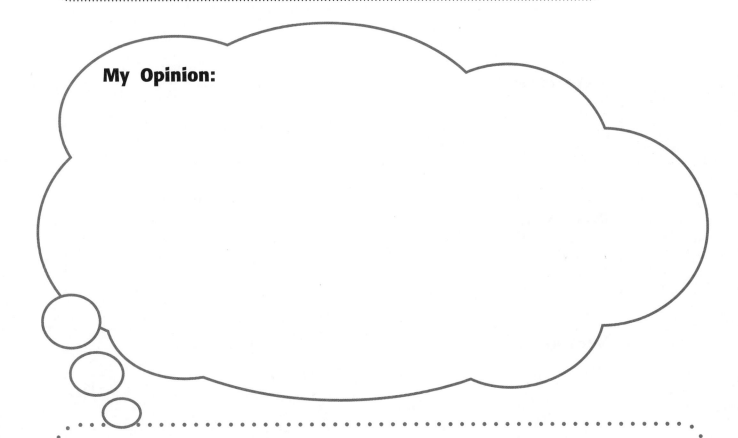

My Opinion:

My Reasons:

COMMON CORE
STATE STANDARDS
W.2.1–
W.2.8

Name_____ Date_____

 Informative/Explanatory Writing Prompt

Explain why Cupcake's journey was amazing. Use details from the text to support your explanation.

Main Idea:
Reason 1: Reason 2: Reason 3:

Name_____ Date_____

Practice 19 Texts with Prompts

COMMON CORE
STATE STANDARDS
**W.2.1–
W.2.8**

Narrative Writing Prompt

Rewrite the story from Cupcake's point of view. Use words such as *I* and *me* to describe what happens and how you feel. Use details from the article.

Beginning:
Middle:
End:

COMMON CORE
STATE STANDARDS
**W.2.1–
W.2.8**

Name_____ Date_____

Read the passage below.

Saturn

1.   Like Earth, Saturn is a planet in our solar system. Saturn is the second-largest planet. Saturn is made up mostly of gases. While it might look solid in pictures, Saturn is more like a cloud.

2.   Earth is the third planet from the sun, and Saturn is the sixth. This means that it takes Saturn longer to orbit, or travel around, the sun. A year is the time it takes a planet to complete one orbit around the sun. A year on Earth is about 365 days. A year on Saturn is about 29 Earth years, or about 10,585 days.

3.   Planets spin while they orbit the sun. The time it takes a planet to make one complete spin is a day. Saturn spins very fast. A day on Earth is 24 hours long. A day on Saturn lasts only 11 hours.

4.   Saturn has more than 50 moons! Eight of these moons are large, and the others are very small. Saturn has rings around it. These rings are not solid. They are made up of ice, dust, and rocks.

Common Core Writing to Texts Grade 2 • ©2014 Newmark Learning, LLC

Name_____ Date_____

COMMON CORE
STATE STANDARDS
W.2.1–
W.2.8

Opinion/Argument Writing Prompt

Do you think scientists know a lot about Saturn? Why or why not? Use details from the text to support your answer.

My Opinion:

My Reasons:

1.

2.

3.

COMMON CORE
STATE STANDARDS
W.2.1–
W.2.8

Name_____ Date_____

Informative/Explanatory Writing Prompt

Explain how Earth and Saturn are alike and how they are different. Use the text to support your explanation.

Earth　　　　**Both**　　　　**Saturn**

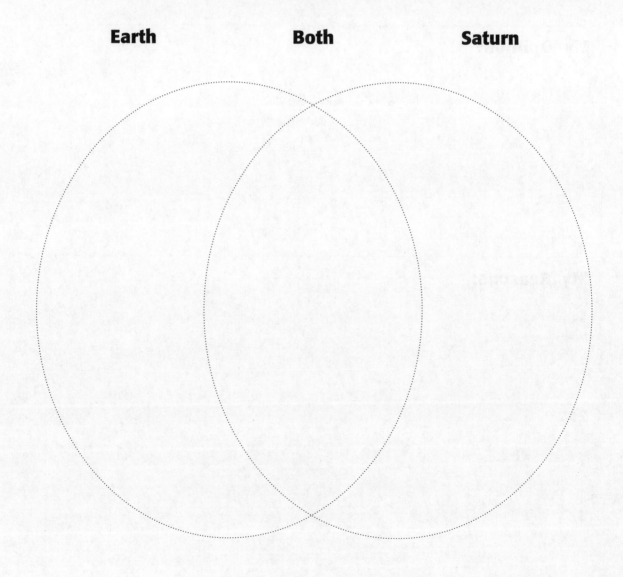

Name_____ Date_____

COMMON CORE
STATE STANDARDS
**W.2.1–
W.2.8**

Narrative Writing Prompt

Imagine that you are on a spaceship that is visiting Saturn. Write a journal entry telling what Saturn is like.

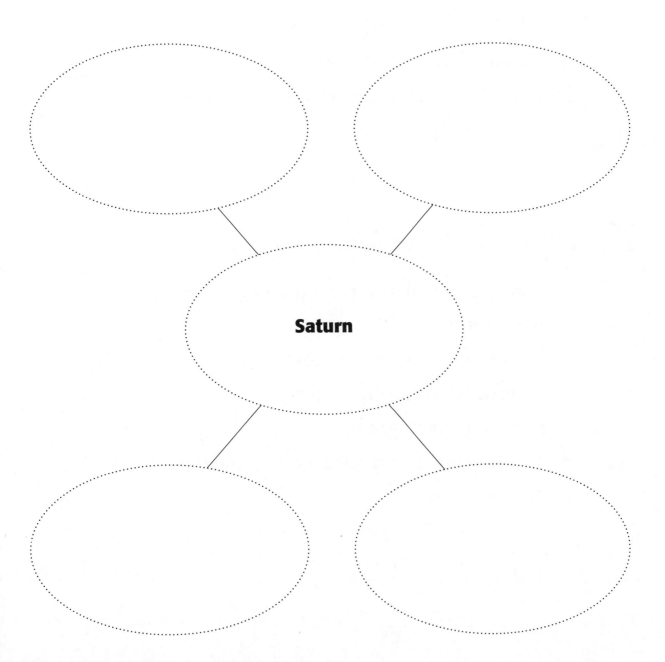

Saturn

COMMON CORE
STATE STANDARDS
**W.2.1–
W.2.5**

Name_____ Date_____

✔ Writing Checklist: Opinion/Argument

❑ I gave the title of the story and the topic.

❑ I stated an opinion.

❑ I gave details from the text to support my opinion.

❑ I used linking words, such as *because*, *and*, and *also*.

❑ I included a strong ending.

❑ I used correct grammar.

❑ I used correct capitalization, punctuation, and spelling.

✔ Writing Checklist: Informative/Explanatory

❑ I introduced the topic and responded to the prompt.

❑ I used facts from the text.

❑ I included a strong ending.

❑ I used correct grammar.

❑ I used correct capitalization, punctuation, and spelling.

COMMON CORE
STATE STANDARDS
**W.2.1–
W.2.5**

Name_____ Date_____

✔ Writing Checklist: Narrative

❏ I gave the title of the story and wrote about one or more events.

❏ I put the events in an order that made sense.

❏ I used time words to show the order.

❏ I included a strong ending.

❏ I used correct grammar.

❏ I used correct capitalization, punctuation, and spelling.

Rubrics and Assessments

Using the Rubrics to Assess Students and Differentiate Instruction

Use the Evaluation Rubrics on the next page to guide your assessment of students' responses. The rubrics are based on the Common Core State Standards for writing. Similar rubrics will be used by evaluators to score new standardized assessments.

After scoring students' writing, refer to the differentiated rubrics on pages 128–133. These are designed to help you differentiate your interactions and instruction to match students' needs. For each score a student receives in the Evaluation Rubrics, responsive prompts are provided to support writers. These gradual-release prompts scaffold writers toward mastery of each writing type.

• For a score of 1, use the Goal Oriented prompts.

• For a score of 2, use the Directive and Corrective Feedback prompts.

• For a score of 3, use the Self-Monitoring and Reflection prompts.

• For a score of 4, use the Validating and Confirming prompts.

Using Technology

If you choose to have students use computers to write and revise their work, consider these ways to support online collaboration and digital publishing:

• Google Drive facilitates collaboration and allows teachers and peers to provide real-time feedback on writing pieces.

• Wikis enable students to share their writing around a common topic.

• Audio tools enable students to record their works (podcasts) for others to hear on a safe sharing platform.

• Student writing can be enriched with images, audio, and video.

Evaluation Rubrics

Student _____ Grade _____

Teacher _____ Date _____

Opinion/Argument				
Traits	**1**	**2**	**3**	**4**
The writer states a strong opinion.				
The writer supplies well-organized reasons that support his or her opinion using facts, concrete examples, and supporting evidence from the text.				
The writer links opinions and reasons using words, phrases, and clauses.				
The writer provides a concluding statement or section.				
The writer demonstrates command of grade-appropriate conventions of standard English.				

Informative/Explanatory				
Traits	**1**	**2**	**3**	**4**
The writer introduces his or her topic with a main idea statement.				
The writer uses facts and details to develop his or her points.				
The writer groups related information together.				
The writer uses linking words and phrases to connect ideas.				
The writer provides a concluding statement or section.				
The writer demonstrates command of grade-appropriate conventions of standard English.				

Narrative				
Traits	**1**	**2**	**3**	**4**
The writer recounts a well-elaborated event or short sequence of events.				
The writer includes dialogue and descriptions of actions, thoughts, and feelings.				
The writer uses temporal words and phrases to signal event order.				
The writer provides a sense of closure to the narrative.				
The writer demonstrates command of grade-appropriate conventions of standard English.				

Key
1–Beginning
2–Developing
3–Accomplished
4–Exemplary

Comments:

Opinion/Argument

TRAITS	1: Goal Oriented
The writer states a strong opinion.	When I start an opinion/argument piece, I state my opinion or point of view. I need to tell exactly what my view is. After reading this prompt, I can state my position as _____.
The writer supplies well-organized reasons that support his or her opinion using facts, concrete examples, and supporting evidence from the text.	I need to think of two or three good reasons to support my opinion. My opinion about this prompt is _____. I'll jot down the evidence I need to support my opinion. Then I'll go back to my writing and include them.
The writer links opinions and reasons using words, phrases, and clauses.	I need to link my reasons together using words and phrases such as *because, therefore, since* and *for example*. I am going to look for places where I can add these words and phrases.
The writer provides a concluding statement or section.	When I finish writing an opinion/argument piece, I need to finish with a strong statement that supports my whole argument. When I conclude this opinion/argument piece, I can restate my position as _____.
The writer demonstrates command of grade-appropriate conventions of standard English.	I am going to read through my writing to make sure that I formed and used both regular and irregular verbs correctly. I will read through my whole opinion/argument piece to make sure that I have spelled words correctly.

2: Directive and Corrective Feedback	3: Self-Monitoring and Reflection	4: Validating and Confirming
Reread the first sentences of your writing. Then go back and reread the prompt. Did you clearly state an opinion that answers the prompt? Revise your statement to make it clear and focused.	Tell me how you chose ____ as your opinion. How can you make your position clearer for the reader?	I can see that your position is ____. You made your opinion very clear. That got me to pay attention to the issue.
What are the reasons for your opinion? Find supporting details and evidence in the text for each reason. Group these ideas together in separate paragraphs.	How did you decide to organize your ideas? Did you identify the information that was most important to include? How did you do this?	You included some strong evidence to support your opinion.
Let's read this paragraph. I see a reason and some evidence. How can you link these ideas together? I notice that you have more than one reason to support your opinion. What words can you add to show the reader that you are moving from one reason to another?	Show me a part of your opinion piece where you link ideas using words and phrases. Show me a part where you could improve your writing by using linking words or phrases.	The words and phrases ____ and ____ are very effective at linking together the connection between your opinions and reasons. They help me understand your ideas.
Reread the last sentences of your opinion/argument piece. Does it end by restating your point of view? Go back and look at your opinion statement. How can you reinforce this idea in your conclusion?	How does your conclusion support your opinion or the position that you have taken? Is there a way you could make this conclusion stronger?	Your concluding section clearly supports your point of view. You've really convinced me that your point of view makes sense.
Read that sentence again. Does it sound right to you? Your noun and verb don't agree. How should you edit that? When you write a title, what do you need to do?	Show me a place in your writing where you used compound and/or complex sentences. Show me a place where you used commas correctly. What rule of punctuation did you apply?	Your opinion/argument piece included many compound sentences, and you remembered where the commas should go. I noticed you spelled many difficult words correctly.

Informative/Explanatory

TRAITS	1: Goal Oriented
The writer introduces his or her topic with a main idea statement.	When I start an informative/explanatory text, I introduce my topic. I'm going to think about what I want my readers to know about _____. Then I create a main idea statement.
The writer uses facts and details to develop his or her points.	I need to find facts and details from the text to support my points. I can go back to the text and underline parts that I think will help my writing. Then I will include them in my informative/explanatory text.
The writer groups related information together.	It is important that I group ideas together in an order that makes sense. I am going to categorize my information to help me structure the parts of my informative/explanatory text.
The writer uses linking words and phrases to connect ideas.	I need to connect my ideas together using linking words, such as *also*, *another*, *and*, *more*, and *but*. I am going to look for places where I can add these words and phrases.
The writer provides a concluding statement or section.	When I finish writing an informative/explanatory text, I need to summarize my ideas in a conclusion. When I conclude, I can look back at my main idea statement, then restate it as _____.
The writer demonstrates command of grade-appropriate conventions of standard English.	I am going to read through my writing to make sure that I used apostrophes to form contractions.

2: Directive and Corrective Feedback	3: Self-Monitoring and Reflection	4: Validating and Confirming
How could you introduce your topic in a way that tells exactly what you will be writing about?	Take a look at your main idea statement. Do you feel that it clearly introduces your topic?	Your main idea statement is clearly _____. That introduction helped me understand exactly what I was going to read about.
What are your main points? Find supporting details and evidence in the text for each point.	Have you included all of the facts you wanted to share about _____?	You included some strong facts, definitions, and details to support your topic.
Put your facts and details into categories. These categories can be the sections of your informative/explanatory text.	How did you decide to organize your ideas? Did you look at an organizing chart? How did it help you?	You organized your informative/explanatory text into [number] well-defined sections.
Let's read this paragraph. I see two related ideas. How can you link these ideas together?	Show me a part of your informative/explanatory text where you could improve your writing by using linking words or phrases.	The words and phrases ____ and ____ are very effective at linking together ideas.
Reread the last sentences of your informative/explanatory text. Do they restate your main idea?	Show me your concluding statement. Is there a way you could make this conclusion stronger?	After I read your conclusion, I felt I had really learned something from your writing.
Read that sentence again. Does it sound right to you? Your verb is not in the right tense. How should you edit that?	Show me a place in your writing where you combined two shorter sentences to make a compound sentence. Where can you combine two sentences to make a longer one?	Your informative/explanatory text included irregular verbs and you remembered how to form them correctly.

Narrative

TRAITS	1: Goal Oriented
The writer recounts a well-elaborated event or short sequence of events.	I will use a sequence of events chart to jot down the events I will write about. I will record details from the text I have already read. I will include those details in my new narrative.
The writer includes dialogue and descriptions of actions, thoughts, and feelings.	I want to include descriptions in my narrative. I will write down words that will help my readers picture what I am writing about. Then I will include these in my narrative.
The writer uses temporal words and phrases to signal event order.	When I write a narrative, I need to use time words so that my reader does not get confused. I will add words and phrases such as *first*, *then*, *the next day*, and *later that week* to help my reader understand the order of events.
The writer provides a sense of closure to the narrative.	I am going to reread the ending of my narrative to make sure that it gives the reader a feeling that the narrative piece is over. I need to concentrate on how the problem in the narrative is solved.
The writer demonstrates command of grade-appropriate conventions of standard English.	I am going to read through my narrative to make sure that I formed and used verbs correctly. I am going to scan through my narrative to make sure I used end punctuation on every sentence.

2: Directive and Corrective Feedback	3: Self-Monitoring and Reflection	4: Validating and Confirming
Think of events that will lead from the problem to the resolution. You've decided to write about _____. Now think of the sequence of events you will include.	What graphic organizer could help you assemble your narrative events? Tell me how you went about organizing your narrative.	The events you organized lead to a [fun, surprising, etc.] resolution.
Imagine that you're a character. What's happening in the narrative? What do you have to say to other characters? What do you have to say about the events?	Show me how you gave information about your characters and setting.	I can visualize where your narrative takes place. You've included some nice descriptive details.
Let's read this paragraph. Is it clear to the reader when all the action is taking place? What words could you add to help the reader's understanding?	Show me where you used time words in your narrative. Show me a place where you could use time words to make the order of events clearer.	The phrase _____ gave a nice transition between ____ and ____.
Let's read the ending of your narrative. Does it show how the problem is solved? Is there something you can add to make sure the reader feels as if the narrative piece is over?	Show me how your ending gives the reader a feeling of closure. Are there any questions from the narrative that you feel were unanswered?	You've developed an interesting resolution to the problem in your narrative. It gives me a sense of closure.
I got confused about the sequence when _____. Take another look at your verb tenses. Make sure they are in the past tense when they should be. When you write a title, what do you need to do?	Show me a place in your writing where your sentences could be better. What could you do to improve them? Show me a sentence in which you changed the punctuation. How did you know it was wrong?	Your narrative included a lot of dialogue, and you used punctuation correctly. I notice you spelled many difficult words correctly!

Editing/Proofreading Symbols

Mark	What It Means	How to Use It
ℓ	Delete. Take something out here.	We went to ~~to~~ the store.
∧	Change or insert letter or word.	San Francico, Calafornia my home.
#	Add a space here.	My family loves to watch baseball.
⌒	Remove space.	We saw the sail boat streak by.
ℓ	Delete and close the space.	I gave the man my monney.
¶	Begin a new paragraph here.	"How are you?" I asked. "Great," said Jack.
⌣	No new paragraph. Keep sentences together.	The other team arrived at one. The game started at once.
∼	Transpose (switch) the letters or words.	Thier friends came with gifts.
≡	Make this a capital letter.	mrs. smith
/	Make this a lowercase letter.	My Sister went to the City.
◯	Spell it out.	Mr. García has 3 cats.
⊙	Insert a period.	We ran home There was no time to spare
∧	Insert a comma.	We flew to Washington D.C.
∨	Insert an apostrophe.	Matts hat looks just like Johns.
∨∨	Insert quotation marks.	Hurry! said Brett.
?	Is this correct? Check it.	The Civil War ended in 1875.
STET	Ignore the edits. Leave as is.	Her hair was brown. STET

134   Common Core Writing to Texts Grade 2 • ©2014 Newmark Learning, LLC

Notes:

Notes: